To: Jynda

All my Gratitude

Lupita Almaraz Aguilar

If The Hat Fits

Poetry by

Lupita Almaraz Aguilar

Table of Contents

Table of Contents

Table of Contents

Table of Contents

Table of Contents

"This work of love is dedicated to my beautiful daughter Nikki Claudette who we loved unconditionally and lost too soon. Thank you for giving us Savanna.

To my beautiful daughters, Jinnelle Veronique and Tommie Marie who I love more than even a poet can express. Thank you for my sweet grandchildren.

And to Roy, the love of my life and sweet husband."

~~ Lupita Almaraz Aguilar

Foreword

I met Lupita in the early 90's. She worked as
a paralegal at a local law firm. We became
immediate friends. Her friendly, happy, and
supportive personality always resonated and
got me in a better mood. This was the case with
everyone with whom she came in contact.

Lupita worked her way through college and law
school, all the while being an exceptional mother
and wife.   I have tremendous respect and
admiration for her numerous accomplishments.

I highly recommend you read her book of
poems. You will quickly connect with Lupita's
unique struggles, triumphs, and life experiences.
You will feel a connection to the Author and will
be able to relate her work to many of your own
life experiences.

It is with great honor I write this foreword to her
book.

~~Scott Humpal,
President, Humpal PT

Prologue

Something in this compilation,
may take you to a destination.

It may fit like the perfect hat,
It may remind you of the past.

Of a love lost or new romance.
It may make you want to dance.

You might just laugh out loud,
You might just cry and shout.

As you read to explore,
Remember, there will always be more.

~~ Lupita Almaraz Aguilar

Chapter 1

If The Hat Fits

The author's collection in this chapter is as its
title suggests – 'If The Hat Fits,' wear it!

If you flatter yourself
With what you see here
Then wear this hat
If it fits you my dear

~~ Lupita Almaraz Aguilar

If The Hat Fits

As the old adage goes
"If the hat fits, wear it!"
If it stings
then it must have some merit.

Like the jabs they delivered
Have backfired now
And they gasp in dismay
As if they just don't know how.

Not everything's about you
But if you care to make it so
We shall not be offended
And we just care not to know.

Be tempered on your own accord
It matters to us none
Because you chose to bicker
You shall remain alone.

If you flatter yourself
With what you see here
Then wear this hat,
If it fits you my dear.

~~ Lupita Almaraz Aguilar

Eloquence

The woman with class
A step above eloquence
Walks in a room
Exuding her elegance
She may be wearing
A Dolce & Gabbana
But it doesn't define her
She's a true Mexicana
Her charisma and poise
Not subtle at all
Everyone sees
Her splendor in awe
But beneath all that beauty
Is more than just grace
An intelligent lady
Running her race
Misunderstood
By her want to be great
She's measured by others
For what to her is innate
Not always so perfect
But striving for that
At times, to a fault
But she makes an impact

~~ Lupita Almaraz Aguilar

Don't Beg

Don't beg him.
He will smell that
like the shark
that swims the ocean
searching for all there is
to fill his insatiable desire.

Don't beg him.
He will discard you
like the fallen leaves
from a tree left to wither
and burn from the sun's fire.

Don't beg him.
He will not come running
like the knight
in shining armor.

Don't beg him.
He will not be true.
He will always be
the deceptive charmer.

Don't beg him.
He is unworthy of the
unconditional love
You carry for him
in spite of his
uncaring demeaner.

Don't beg him.
Your desperate emotions
are temporary.
Release yourself
from that inferior.

~~ Lupita Almaraz Aguilar

Like Butter Without Toast

You're put together

You seem secure

At times objective

But then unsure

You feel indifferent

Not routine

Quick to judge

What you haven't seen

Sometimes slow

Sometimes fast

Today was great

But did not last

That's a day

In the life of most

Like having butter

Without the toast

~~Lupita Almaraz Aguilar

Lion in the Den

He did it. Not me.

Yet here I am confused.

He has a way of doing this

Now I'm the one accused.

Don't know quite how that happens

But he's really good at that.

He tells me that I'm crazy

He pounces like a cat.

But I'm the lion in this den

And I'll eat that pussy cat.

Go find a mouse somewhere

That let's you play like that.

~~ Lupita Almaraz Aguilar

Me Too

Look at these fools
Thinking they could
Take a piece of a woman
With nothing to lose.

Thought they'd be spared
And all would be good
Now they run scared
Denying the truth.

They never imagined
The women would speak
They took full advantage
Thought women were weak.

Women are strong
And they're ready to tell
What all these men did
And they're ringing the bell.

Will you be next?
Is the question to ask.
Looking over your shoulder
Until the day you're unmasked?

~~ Lupita Almaraz Aguilar

Misunderstood

She believes in undying love

Never giving up

She loves unconditionally

Her passion for her family is unwavering

Her instinct to protect interferes

with the perception that she is overbearing

She is often misunderstood.

~~ Lupita Almaraz Aguilar

No Desire

When there is no more desire

to be with only the one who loves

him most

because he wants for the company

of any other,

it must be time to be done.

Because there was once a time

when any other was unwanted

owing to his desire

to be with only the one

whom he loved most.

~~ Lupita Almaraz Aguilar

Resurrected

Beneath the surface
lurk the burning embers -
the ones you so viciously lit.
You think that no one remembers
the curse of your violent fit.

The pain you delivered - relentless.
The terror you brought took its toll.
You ravaged my innocence then.
Destroyed what I thought of this world.

I used to wander this earth
Lost, excluded, and disconnected.
But then, like the butterfly from a caterpillar,
my transformation slowly resurrected.

Your presence is unwelcome here.
My freedom has surpassed you and
I am disassociated from your hold.
You are irrelevant to everything that is me.
Peace and courage are my new norm.

~~ Lupita Almaraz Aguilar

Scoundrels

I've seen a lot of good movies

And read a bunch of great books

I've seen a whole lot of heroes

And can pick out as many crooks

Friends aren't a dime a dozen

But scoundrels are everywhere

They'll come in at every angle

They don't care to play unfair

The nicest of them aren't all kind

They slither their way in the door

Arriving to take what they came for

And then coming back for some more

The warnings are not always clear

It could be who you least expect

But scoundrels will be exposed

They seldom have no respect

~~ Lupita Almaraz Aguilar

She Knows

You broke your promise of love.

Then you told the whole world.

How could you do this to her?

Why did you cause such a whirl?

Why did you want to leave?

She has not healed from that pain.

How could you've made such a fuss?

She has never felt so much shame.

You think that she doesn't know,

But your reasons don't carry much weight.

She knows what you have denied,

She just chooses not to berate.

You dismissed what you did

But your mess lingers still.

You were selfish and foolish

And you swallowed that pill.

~~ Lupita Almaraz Aguilar

Smear

When the underlying story
Takes a slight detour
The delivery will differ
If the intent is to obscure

Once it rolls the tongue
And into someone's ear
You cannot disassemble
The defect of the smear

Although retractions might arise
The damage has been done
Thus the underlying story
Has taken a new turn

Now a different explanation
Of what she meant to say
Will tarnish reputations
And resonate betray

Reducing the whole story
To nothing but a lie
Lost all its credibility
of keeping it alive

~~ Lupita Almaraz Aguilar

Whatever It Takes

Walk the big walk
Talk the big talk
Whatever it takes
She is a rock

No challenge too large
No hours too long
Whatever it takes
This woman is strong

Leading the leaders
Breaking the mold
Whatever it takes
Delivers like gold

Knows to take charge
Pressure or not
Whatever it takes
She is on top

Making a change
Fearless and bold
Whatever it takes
She's in control

~~ Lupita Almaraz Aguilar

That Speak

If you step into someone's abode

You should be kind at least

It really is appalling

To behave just like a beast

It is also quite unpleasant

To hear profanatory speak

The derogatory rambling

That can make a sailor shriek

The disregard for others

Clearly on display

And if you point it out

Be ready for the rage

It cannot be the norm

That you turn the other cheek

Just because it has become

The way some people speak

~~Lupita Almaraz Aguilar

The Trouble with Couples

Couples have trouble communicating.

Each one thinks they are right.

Couples have their own opinions,

then, comes the big ugly fight.

Neither wants to say they're sorry,

for fear of losing their side.

Much rather sink to the bottom,

than risk losing their pride.

Some can go on for days,

without so much as a word,

pretending the other's invisible

choosing not to be heard.

Others may dangerously rumble,

possibly worst of its kind.

Some may just move right along,

carelessly thinking they're fine.

The trouble with couples is later,

when all has gone bitterly wrong,

neither is willing to say it,

and now the couple is done.

~~Lupita Almaraz Aguilar

Unaware

She sees his angst

His petulance

His arrogance

His uncertainty

She stays

She tolerates

She believes

He doesn't see

Her determination

Her willingness

Her certainty

He leaves

~~Lupita Almaraz Aguilar

Taste My Powder

If you taste my powder,
I will capture you.
Unsuspecting, you will indulge
and your heart
will belong to me.
You will love me
more than any other
or anything.

We will indulge together.
I will not let you go.
If you taste my powder,
you will fear no more.
I will give you courage
like you have never known.
Even if it is temporary,
I will not leave you alone.

I will nudge you
to taste my powder.
I will be your constant reminder.
You will not need money,
friends, family, or a partner.
We will embrace each other.
If you drop me like a bad habit,
I will be here waiting forever.
If you taste my powder.

~~ Lupita Almaraz Aguilar

Tall Tale

If you heard a different version

Of what really happened here

I cannot change their story

But mine is crystal clear

They feel compelled to repeat it

There's a reason why

They're trying to convince themselves

But they can't escape the lies

If you really listen closely

You see my truth prevails

But if you choose their story

Perhaps you like tall tales

~~ Lupita Almaraz Aguilar

Don't Ruffle the Feathers

Don't ruffle the feathers,
You say.
Ignore their behavior and we'll be okay.
Others will think we are like them,
You claim.
Let's just forget what they did
to our name.
Don't add fuel to the fire they lit.
Let it be!
It's all in the past and they're gone.
Can't you see?

The feathers were ruffled for much too long
What they did and they said
is more than just wrong.
How many times does it take
for you to see
that the pain they have caused
has cut really deep?
that you feel more important
what others might say
is compelling no doubt
with a sense of betray.
You claim not to choose sides but you have.
It should be quite clear and it's sad.

~~ Lupita Almaraz Aguilar

You Forgot

I felt I was falling apart

When you were ready to leave

Because you thought I was flawed

And you said all those things about me

You said I got lost from the trauma

And you were ready to run

You focused on all of the drama

Announcing that you were done

You forgot to care for our love

To nurture, to listen, and hear

You suddenly said, "That's enough-

I just don't want to be here!"

You forgot who was there for you most

How I always took care of your needs

How I cared despite all your faults

How I helped you with all of your deeds

You forgot that I carried the weight

And were hurt when I mentioned this fact

You forgot that I do not forget

I know you were taken aback.

May you never be granted the day

When I'm free to break my silence.

~~ Lupita Almaraz Aguilar

Chapter 2

Where There is Love

The author's collection in this chapter is
of course about the most poetic discussion
— Love — in all of its splendor and consequence.

It does appear
That she will take
Her secret to her grave
And none the wiser
Of her deceit
Their souls
She did not save.

~~ *Lupita Almaraz Aguilar*

Dignified

He asks if she will join
in a friendly skinny dip.
And if I'm not as skinny as you wish?
She replies.
I beg your pardon ma'am,
whatever do you mean?
A skinny dip has nothing to do with size.
She takes a moment to reflect
and courteously declines.

He then suggests a walk
along the sandy beach.
And if my legs are not appealing?
I think - Sir - you overreach.

Madam, a walk would not require
any leg-appeal.
But if you'd rather,
we can simply sip some tea in here.
And if my sipping is too loud?
I will be mortified!
There shall not be a thing to do
unless it will be dignified.

Well then, I can take you to the alter
and marry you at once.
For there is not a thing more dignified
than making you my wife.
She gasps in all her splendor and
requests a wedding song.
I shall be yours today and for the rest of
our lives.

He had no idea why she eagerly agreed,
and to his great confusion,
she was not a bit discreet.
She took his hand in hers
and as they walked along,
She said, "My ring can be of any sort,
so long as we are one."

~~Lupita Almaraz Aguilar

None The Wiser

Two love one,
The one loves two.
The trio in despair.
They fall for her
But both are unaware.
None the wiser
Of their love of her
Nor, that the other cares.
But she just carries on
Pursuing the affair.
It does appear
That she will take
Her secret to her grave,
And none the wiser
Of her deceit,
Their souls
She did not save.

~~ Lupita Almaraz Aguilar

Nothing

How many times does her heart have to break

How many times must she cry

What's all the reason behind it

Why does she keep up the lie

Why does he make her unhappy

Why must it be so unfair

One day he tells her he loves her

And the next he just doesn't care

Her heart is desperate and foolish

And it's dying as each day goes by

The love she'd been wanting to give him

Can't be shared if he won't even try

She's been longing to tell him she loves him

She's been longing to hold him so tight

But each time that she tries – he rejects it

And he constantly puts up a fight

She can't try to hold on to nothing

When nothing can't see what she feels

And trying to hold on to him

Is the nothing that's becoming surreal

~~ Lupita Almaraz Aguilar

Heartbreak Museum

It is most tumultuous
To find entanglement
In the heartbreak of many
In full display for all to see
The wondering
The whispering
The unending inquiry

The conflict of the heartbreak
The unknown
The passion and
The dread
In full exhibition
For the spectator
To assemble in his mind
All that may have been said

~~Lupita Almaraz Aguilar

Hidden Love

She wonders if he really loves her

She loves him more each day

And when she sees him, she sighs

She never knows what to say

It's just a feeling

She can't explain

A feeling of love that

She cannot feign

It's a beautiful feeling

Only she holds

But her feelings for him

Can never unfold

~~ Lupita Almaraz Aguilar

I Long

I long to hear your footsteps

Come walking through my door

And I want to see your smile

At least just this once more

I long for you to hug me

And hold me in the night

So here I am just waiting

Still thinking that you might

I long to hear your whispers

And how you used to say

That you loved me truly

But that was yesterday

I long for us to be in love

And how it used to be

I remember it was both of us

But then you set us free

~~ Lupita Almaraz Aguilar

I Overheard Your Conversation

My friends told me that you called
So I tried to call you back
And as I picked up the receiver
I recognized your voice and laugh

You hadn't realized it
But your phone was off the line
And when I heard what you were saying
I couldn't help but start to cry

I heard you say you didn't love me
I heard you say you didn't care
And when I tried to call next door
They said you were not there

I feel shame and I feel anger
I feel cheated and betrayed
And although I've heard you say it
I know exactly what I'll say

I'll say what I have said
So many times before
I'll say that I still love you
I'll forgive you this once more

~~ Lupita Almaraz Aguilar

Break-Up List

It has come to an end

Find my best friend

Cannot go back

Put all his things in a sack

Leave fast and change my number

Stay busy to fight the somber

Cry loud but avoid the drama

Call sister — call momma

Be strong and take charge

Now's the time to live large

Sell all things that were ours

Do not count the hours

Be brave and stay cool

Do not act like a fool

Do not wither — do not break

Dance a lot and sleep late

~~ Lupita Almaraz Aguilar

Still Waiting

I think of the way we used to be

I think of the good times we had

I'm sitting here feeling sorry

I know this is just so sad

Every day I can see his smile

Then slowly it fades away

Telling myself he's gone now

Yet I'll be waiting another day

I'll wait like I've done in the past

Maybe he'll come back to me

I'll wait here and maybe he'll call

Will he reach out to me?

~~ Lupita Almaraz Aguilar

Is It Love?

Could it be happening

Could this be true

I think I'm in love

Don't know what to do

Could it be so

Is there a chance

Is this puppy love

Or serious romance

What happens next

How do I know

What must I do

Does all of this show?

~~ Lupita Almaraz Aguilar

It's Over

The together part is over,

She loved him more than she should.

Part of her is hurting,

She never thought he would.

She tries to hide her pain

Doesn't know where to start.

Because he said it's over

It is time for us to part

Her racing thoughts of loneliness

The feeling of loss she holds.

It hurts to know she lost him,

There's nothing more to be told.

~~ Lupita Almaraz Aguilar

Mom

I love that you are my mom
You were always by my side
You wiped the tears I shed
And made me smile when I cried

I love you for showing me love
For teaching me to be strong
I love you because you are my mother
And holding my hand all along

~~ Lupita Almaraz Aguilar

Not My Love

I know you do not love me
The way that I love you
I know you do not want me
Near as much the way I do
Thought that I could beg my way
And that somehow in due time
You'd love me just as much
And we would be just fine
It's time to say goodbye
I've tried the hardest that I could
I cannot sit and wonder
If someday you'll love me too

~~ Lupita Almaraz Aguilar

Promise Ring

With this ring I do promise

To forever love you true

And I want for you to love me

The same way I love you

I want us both to share our thoughts

And always feel our touch

With this ring I do promise

To love you very much

~~ Lupita Almaraz Aguilar

Got Burned

She loved him once

But not again

She must be done

It has to end

Her heart is broken

Turned to mush

The laughter gone

Her world is crushed

She played with fire

And then got burned

He had another

She had learned

No questions asked

She could've known

Chose not to see

And then got burned

~~ Lupita Almaraz Aguilar

Too Late

Once I needed you

That once you told me no

It didn't feel so good

Just to see you go

Now you say you need me

Well I don't think it's true

Now you say you love me

It's too bad I don't love you

~~ Lupita Almaraz Aguilar

Yesterday's Regrets

It was all about you

The dream I had last night

All the sweet warm kisses

Everything seemed right

But today I called again

You had not been home

Just another clue

That you were not alone

My dreams are dying slowly

My heart will have to mend

All the bitter memories

Are yesterday's regrets

~~ Lupita Almaraz Aguilar

A Valentine's Day Aftermath

All the love she gave
was not enough.
He did not return that night.
The red roses he sent her
had a note he did not write.

The mistress of the moment
told her all that he had done.
It was a Valentine's Day aftermath
when the betrayal had begun.

She took the flowers and the note
with his belongings to a fire.
It was swift and without warning,
and she was left without desire.

~~Lupita Almaraz Aguilar

I See You

I like your smile

The way you walk

To hear you laugh

To hear you talk

I see you

The funny looks

The laughs out loud

The way you hate

To be in crowds

I see you

When you're not there

I love your quirks

The way you care

~~ Lupita Almaraz Aguilar

You Used To Open My Door

I know now it's not like before

You used to see me

And open my door

But it's not like that anymore

I do recall the days

When you would say

How much you loved me

And you'd never leave

But I know now

It's not like before

When you used to open my door

~~ Lupita Almaraz Aguilar

Chapter 3

Laugh Out Loud

The author's collection in this chapter is very much a fun-spirited version of what most love to experience — laughter. As funny and unbelievable as they may seem, many of these pieces are some version of actual events.

My heart is crumbling
Like a pan-de-polvo
Because we were together
But now we're over

~~ Lupita Almaraz Aguilar

Laugh Out Loud

If the world had more of you

It would be a bucket of laughs

Most everything you say or do

Is an unintentional gaffe

Not one with a mere distraction

But more like a scandalous wit

The more that you say or do

the more comical it can get

Your quick-witted talk leaves them rolling

Maybe their eyes or their belly

But either opinion will have to admit

That laughter appeals to so many

Who does not like a good "laugh-out-loud"

The kind that can leave us breathless

If you can deliver that kind of laugh

Let that laughter be endless.

~~ Lupita Almaraz Aguilar

A Little Difference

We have aunties and uncles
Who we call tias and tios
We may listen to classical music
But also love corridos and gritos

We may set the table with linen
But can eat wherever we land
We may use utensils and china
Other times, just tortillas and our hands

We might eat steak and potatoes
But love enchiladas and rice
We may have breakfast in bed
Or we'll eat our tacos outside

Might take a girl to the opera
Then take her out to the lake
And fancy or not at this outing
It'll make for a fabulous date!

~~ Lupita Almaraz Aguilar

Back Then

Back then we used to play outdoors
We skipped and jumped and such
Didn't twiddle with our thumbs
We weren't allowed to do that much

Ran around on our bare feet
We didn't feel the thorns
Seldom did we care
If shoes were even worn

All the neighbors' kids hung out
We really broke a sweat
Our brothers' competition
was jumping over our fence

Our swimming pools were charcos
We didn't mind the mud
We simply used the outdoor hose
To wash off all the crud

Our track was our caliche road
Where we often held a race
We scraped our knees and elbows
It was an awesome place

~~ *Lupita Almaraz Aguilar*

Balcony Lady

The lady on the balcony
Would study there each day
For hours upon hours
She wouldn't leave that place

All alone indulging
In the study of the law
Reading through the night
So many tears she fought

The long unending hours
Sometimes were hard to bear
Her only outing was the balcony
Where she would get some air

She sat there much too often
Her neighbors often friendly -
Would pause for just a moment
To converse with the balcony lady

Determined to pursue her goal
She read in silence and aloud
Tirelessly writing, then more reading
But no visitors allowed

Her dedication drowned her sorrow
The harder it got the more she tried
When the balcony lady was done
her neighbors clapped and cried

~~ Lupita Almaraz Aguilar

Clumsy

Laughter is good medicine
So the saying goes
Even when you trip and fall
Or stub your little toe

But it's not all that funny
When the toe belongs to you
Or when that little fall
Leaves you black and blue

The clumsiness is cute and all
Unless you catch your heel
Then all those words you shouldn't say
Come spewing out the reel

Your hair gets caught and tangled up
And as you try so hard to pull
The only thing you're thinking then
Is how you're not so cool

When out the door you rush
Because you're running late
You think you might just make it
And then you hit the gate

Yes it might just make you giggle
At the master of disaster
But when it's you who's clumsy
It's not quite a laughing matter

Laugh anyway.

~~ Lupita Almaraz Aguilar

Coffee Brown

It was but a normal evening
With some siblings sitting home
When arrive the elder aunts and uncles
And Fancy Aunt arrives alone

One elder uncle begins to flirt
With Fancy Aunt, oh my
Because his wife was not around
He thought he would by sly

He asked Fancy out for coffee
But it was much too late
When Fancy Aunt rebuked him
He knew there was no date

The laughter of that moment
Was just a burst so loud
But then, the other uncle
Thought he too could be so proud

And to his own amazement
He spoke his thoughts aloud
He dotes about the Fancy Aunt
And then .. there was one sound

His wife's heels slowly walking
Clear across that living room
She stands square before her husband
And slaps him hard - it's true!

His cheeks shook all about - they did
like the blubber of a whale
And everyone just sat there
As he turned a little pale

The nieces quickly ran
to tell what just happened there
And left one nephew all alone
Sitting quiet in his chair

Well, Uncle couldn't help himself
So found the courage to say
Do not alarm yourself
This is how we like to play

From this eventful evening
We now call COFFEE BROWN
Has turned up so much laughter
He will never live it down!

~~ Lupita Almaraz Aguilar

113

The Wallet

There was a little wallet

Whose name was Brownie Mallet

She lived in a little pocket

But she would never lock it

The poor thing fell out one day

And I recall it was the first of May

She prayed to God that she'd be found

Or she would no more weigh a pound

Then two best friends were walking home

And came across a wallet

They found her laying on the ground

And rescued Brownie Mallet.

~~ Lupita Almaraz Aguilar

Ni Modo

Mexican moms can be funny
Make bad situations satire
If you come home crying, she'll say,
"Ni modo, don't be playing with fire."
Mexican moms have a come-back
For falling and scraping your knees,
"Didn't I tell you and Rozie
Not to be climbing the trees?"

When you're moping around feeling sad
She'll send you to clean all the floors
No inuendo, no caution
The sadder you get, the more chores.
You tell her your boyfriend just left you
And you just don't know what to do.
She'll say, "Pos, ni modo, I told you
not to be dating that sonso!"

Do not expect to be pampered
No time for dealing with that.
She'll then call your tia to tell her
That you actually cried for that rat.
If you get upset that she gossiped
Ni modo, you don't stand a chance.
Don't be sharing your feelings
No time for that song and dance.

~~ Lupita Almaraz Aguilar

Mexican Love

My heart is crumbling
Like a pan-de-polvo
Because we were together
But now we're over

Remember all those times you cared
You used to make me buñuelos
Well, now it's changed around
And all I have are marshmallows

I wish you felt the way you did
When you made those bean tamales
Those were the best of times
But now I just eat my picante

You think I'm okay but I'm not
I miss your Mexican food
The buttered tortillas you made
Those tacos were really that good.

~~ Lupita Almaraz Aguilar

Monkey Business

The client calls and quickly begins to talk,
"The cops are looking for me," he says in shock.
I listen closely for all the clues
But he blurts his words and seems confused.
"I picked up a monkey on the side of the road."

I then pause for a moment as I think it's a prank
But the man – yes, the man – speaks frank.
"I picked up a monkey on the side of the road,
and the cops think I took it from somebody's home."

I pause once more trying to really listen
for any clue of voice recognition,
but it was no one I knew.

So I took some more notes and further inquired.
He continued to speak,
"I took it to my moms, but the monkey went wild."
"My mom got upset and told me to go,
so I took the monkey back to the road."
Yes...the road...where he'd found it, he said.

I put him on hold to keep my composure,
I COULDN'T imagine this man was kosher.
He was.

He thought it was cute but his kids were afraid.
I couldn't believe what this man had just said.
So his mom insisted he take it out of the home.
He took it back to the side of the road.

Then I took a deep breath and unwillingly asked,
Why he left a monkey on the side of a road.
The man candidly said,
"Well, that's where I found it, so back there it goes!"

~~ Lupita Almaraz Aguilar

New Size Six

Fashion moguls look at me
So much thinner than I see me.
Their size twelve is the new size six.
Now we know why nothing fits.

Stiletto shoes that kill the feet,
Crunch your toes and leave you beat.
Try your size and you will bulge.
Fashion bigwigs won't divulge.

The runway model wears size zero,
Rules the catwalk like a fashion hero.
I walk the hallway in that manner,
It's quite a spectacle without the glamour.

The sleek designer of haute couture
Can make my wardrobe feel insecure.
So out of touch with the current trend,
But with my knockoff I will pretend.

~~Lupita Almaraz Aguilar

Purple Pants

She knew she'd seen him before

When he asked if she would dance

She couldn't remember where

But remembered his purple pants

Then while the two were chatting

He mentioned the little store

She giggled and then he whispered

The color of dress she wore

She couldn't contain herself

The flatter was just too cute

The boy with the purple pants

Was dancing without his boots

~~ Lupita Almaraz Aguilar

Small Town

We lived large
In a very small home.
Grew up small-town,
One of the largest families around.
Best Father. Greatest mother.
Seven sisters, Five brothers.

Gathered often,
Laughed aloud.
Great times.
Big crowds.
Kids played "bote quemado,"
Ran fast,
Jumped rope,
Had a blast.

Sang songs we couldn't sing,
But didn't care at all.
Because dancing was our thing,
Every weekend at the Ball!
Well - quinceañeras -
Hosted plenty. Attended most.
Danced cumbias and huapangos.

Didn't have a lot of dough,
But mom custom-made our clothes.
Our Dad worked hard,
Gave us what we needed most.

We lived large
In a very small home.
Didn't take a train.
Never went to Rome.

~~ Lupita Almaraz Aguilar

The Laugh

Ever think you have a funny laugh
So, when you laugh they laugh at you,
And what may be funny at the time
is not funnier than you?

A laugh has many faces
and many different sounds.
Some will look quite dainty
While others look like clowns.

The donkey laugh, the cackle,
The belly-burst is best
The snicker - not so nice,
And the snort beats all the rest.

The howl and the roar
are quite the crazy laughing pair,
'Cause when you hear those two
The crowd will stop and stare.

The giggle and the chuckle
Can become a cachinnation.
Then all the clapping starts,
and we have a standing ovation.

The hee-haw and the haw-haw
Are both one in the same.
But the titter is no match for
the one they call the bray.

~~Lupita Almaraz Aguilar

Dream

In my sleep,

I am dreaming of all things grand.

I am Queen and my King is Shrek

All of its sequence is fickle,

because that's how dreams manifest.

My lovely dress becomes tangled

As I ride my horse through the mud.

I am barefoot in the forest.

and it is raining glittered suds.

I cannot find the door.

It is hidden behind a tiny brick wall.

My Shrek has come to my rescue.

He is green, thin, and very tall.

My horse is now a mastiff.

I had one long ago.

He bites my King.

I awake, barking at the floor.

~~ Lupita Almaraz Aguilar

Then Comes Marriage

First date looks so good

Her hair pinned up and his looks cool

Her short skirt and stiletto heels

His leather jacket was not a steal

Picked her up in his shiny car

Cruising at night, under the stars

All alone on this perfect night

Fancy dinner by candlelight

Flirting, dancing, romantic stare

The night is young. They don't care

But then, reality comes on board

They get married and that's no more

The kids are awake running amuck

And now he drives a clunky old truck

His leather jacket is now faux pas

She can barely afford a bra

No more alone time or perfect nights

The children are screaming and starting a fight

~~ Lupita Almaraz Aguilar

Thirsty Thursday

He takes one sip
The night is young
The tone is set
It has begun

It's 'Thirsty Thursday'
Friends arrive
Another sip
And a big high five

They're blabbing on
This, this, and that
I have a huge
Five-acre ranch

Another gulp
And then
He can't pronounce
His name

They stay the course
Catch bigger fish
More drinks will come
They're on the brink

They're walking crooked
Slurring words
Telling stories
They've told before

But it's 'Thirsty Thursday'
So, they drink some more
Now, way past midnight.
But they still won't go

They make no sense
Think they're cool
Not so brave
Is the drunken fool

~~ Lupita Almaraz Aguilar

Diet

I'm not too fond of a diet

Don't see how anyone is

You start out with all of your gumption

Then out of that diet you fizz

We'll do it together and calorie count

We'll take on the world you will see

Then after a week when you lost half a pound

It's - who will have ice cream with me

I once could eat all the twinkies

And cake was no problem at all

Now, even if I just say, "sugar"

The pounds come running along

Exhausting to read all the contents

Of each single food that you eat

For the grams, and the fat, and the carbs

Have already delivered defeat

~~ Lupita Almaraz Aguilar

Grumpy

Grumpy much?
We can feel your mood.
Though you might think not,
It can cause a feud.
Your eyebrows cringed
as you walk around.
Your mouth exuding
its biggest frown.
You walk the walk
of a mean old grump.
But talk the talk
of a wimpy chump.

~~ Lupita Almaraz Aguilar

Wedding Blunder

Walking up the isle
She trips and tears her dress
The groom runs to her rescue
But laughs at all her mess

He tries to lift her gently
But he's clumsier than her
He stumbles as he tries
But he causes such a stir

The preacher takes a step
But as he turns to look
He spills the holy water
And along he joins the groom

Everyone is laughing now
The bridesmaids start a chant
The choir sings a rock song
And the groomsmen start to dance

The wedding vows still happen
Bride and groom a tad disheveled
No one cared at all
It was the best one ever!

~~Lupita Almaraz Aguilar

Chapter 4

All The Broken Pieces

Savanna Aguilar is the Author's granddaughter,
and the daughter of their late Nikki — to whom
this chapter is dedicated.

The author's collection in this chapter is mostly a compilation of
writings about the loss of her very young daughter, Nikki.
Some of the pieces are deep and heart-wrenching.

I cannot share the burden
as it is much too
demanding - unforgiving - unbearable

~~ Lupita Almaraz Aguilar

Fragments

Who would have thought you'd fly like an Angel.

Never dreamed you would leave us so soon.

Your sweet child asked,

Why her mommy was not in her room.

She had so many questions -

May have answered a few.

Don't quite recall what they were,

But I'm sure I did not tell the truth.

So many fragmented details,

Yet some are embedded no doubt.

Have yet to find any courage

To say what happened out loud.

Everyone asks the same question,

What happened to her and then why.

Each time, the response is the same

a gut-wrenching breath and a sigh.

Somehow a whisper emerges.

Don't want to answer at all.

The gasp, the confusion, the sorrow

Wish they had not asked at all.

~~Lupita Almaraz Aguilar

Another Year Without Her

So another year
without her
Is like a pain unknown.
My entire body - heavy.
My grief seems to have grown
My world seems so tiny
I want to cringe and crumble.
But I can't.
I can't because I can't.
My sadness is so thick
I have trouble breathing
I can't speak.
I cried.
I am immobile.
I struggle to move forward -
Some days I struggle
More than others.
Today I struggle
Like a mother who
Lost her beautiful daughter.
I hope you never know this pain.
I will never be able to express
The trauma
The fear
The pain
The confusion
The conflict within
I will never be able to explain
the different Me.
I love you more than I can say.

~~ Lupita Almaraz Aguilar
July 11, 2017 (8 years)

Tacenda

Hush, it shall be left unspoken

You cannot say,

You must not say.

It is bound to leave her broken—

All of that past just doesn't matter.

You cannot tell,

You must not tell.

It is certain to leave her shattered—

Best let that go and keep it silent.

You cannot speak,

You must not speak.

Her mind will perpetuate violence.

~~ Lupita Almaraz Aguilar

Rewrite This Story

If she could rewrite this story

She would want to go back in time

She might not have tried to dismiss

What scared her about all the signs

She'd try something different this time

Seek out more help from another

She would carry her longer than usual

She'd do more than the previous mother

She'd uncover all that was hidden

Try to decipher the truth

Try harder to untangle the mess

She'd do more than she did if she could

~~ Lupita Almaraz Aguilar

Anxiety Has Many Friends

Anxiety has many friends,

It seldom lets you rest.

It follows you to celebrations.

It partners with frustrations.

It cleverly knows your every move,

then lurks beneath your moods.

Anxiety is unpredictable.

It shows up with Mr. Despicable.

Anxiety needs no introduction.

It creates its own production,

and is a master of destruction.

~~Lupita Alamaraz Aguilar

Be Good With Me

I am reminded of her daily

Please do not ask

Just be good with me

My words are thick

I cannot speak

Each time I think of her

I see her pretty face

In all the empty space

Because I do remember

I built a shield

No one can see

I miss her so

Be good with me

~~ Lupita Almaraz Aguilar

Because I Am Her Mother

Before today - I thought I knew. I knew nothing.
I knew my pain, but it pales in comparison
to the pain she knew.
I know her pain now, but I cannot speak it.
I imagine her world but I refuse it.
Because I am her mother, I cannot share it.
I used to think I tried, but not like she did.
I might have thought I did,
but I could not have known her struggle -
how much she cared, or
how determined she was in her battle.
No one can begin to know her sorrow,
her thoughts, her hope, her conviction -
and what she felt....
This is not guilt, it's a rude awakening.
Because we do not understand -
we shun, we blame, we judge.
When someone is ill, we run to aid
When someone's mind is ill - we run away.
I sit and cry and I will shed these tears forever,
but my sweet child cries no more
and for that - I must be grateful

"God didn't bring me this far just to drop me"
I read these words in her diary
and they are inscribed on her stone........
Mom

~~Lupita Almaraz Aguilar

Desolation

Having lost discernment
She sunk deep into despair
Could almost see demise
Lost her will to care

All alone with others
Who could not see her battle
The constant aching struggle
That awful state of fragile

Too deep to speak aloud
The agonizing thoughts
No matter what she did
She was all tied up in knots

Nobody knew her world
The crippling days and nights
The constant desolation
The internal crushing fight

~~ Lupita Almaraz Aguilar

Desperation

The feeling of desperation

Wanting something that might not be

The hope you can make it right

That's the trouble here you see

You try, but can't find the strength

Thinking that you're so close

Confusion sets in again

And nobody really knows

The feeling of desperation

Uncertain of what was said

Repeatedly asking yourself

What really happened today?

~~Lupita Almaraz Aguilar

Figment

In her mind you are real
In her heart, she can feel
She is happy that you care
But you don't. You're not there
She knows not that you're gone
She believes but you do not
Because there never has been you
But she believes you to be true

~~Lupita Almaraz Aguilar

I Cry Again

I cannot sleep again
I think I will be able, but I cannot
I cry again,
I cry alone again
I cannot wake someone to tell
that I am crying again
I cannot at least complain
because my pain cannot compare to hers
I miss her so much,
and I cry again
This is like nothing I have ever known
nothing more unforgiving,
nothing more unbearable - ever
I see her every single day
in something, in someone, in everything
I cannot share this feeling - the depth of it
I will not share it
as I dare not permit another to feel what I feel
I cannot share the burden
as it is much too
demanding - unforgiving - unbearable
these words are too simple
to grasp the true depth
of the emotion -
it is impossible
I will never, ever, be the same
I may seem so, but I am not.
I love my child unconditionally -
I am certain.

~~ Lupita Almaraz Aguilar

I'll Always Remember

I think of you often

Imagine your smile

Your kindness

Your amazing style

The long hours you spent on your hair

Your shyness

Your quirks

How much you cared

Making everyone smile with you

The outbursts of your laughter

The warmth of your hands

The before and after

~~ Lupita Almaraz Aguilar

It Wasn't You

She knows that you are hurting
She can see it in your eyes
She also knows that feeling
When someone says goodbye
The betrayal by another
Is quite hard to understand
It wasn't you she didn't want
It was the torment she couldn't stand

~~ Lupita Almaraz Aguilar

Fog

There once was a time

When I couldn't see

When the fog was too thick

When I couldn't breathe

The grass wasn't green

The sky slightly grey

I walked through a tunnel

Nothing but haze

Afraid to be seen

Slow motion was fast

Walked all alone

Became an outcast

~~ Lupita Almaraz Aguilar

Numb

The sleepless nights are grueling

But not more so than all the grief

The numbness makes me wonder

If I'm in is serious disbelief.

The most peculiar thing is how

I have managed to survive it – HOW?

As I step out of myself, looking in

It seems unimaginably unbearable.

Looking out—seems even stranger than I feel.

Some say that I am strong

and they could never understand

How it is that I am me.

I have no explanation other than

I cannot see. I cannot see that I am me.

How does one do this?

How does a mother survive without her child?

I swore I never could. I knew I never could.

Yet somehow I have, but I have not.

How will I keep my composure?

~~Lupita Almaraz Aguilar

Only God Knows

This tragedy has hit us,
Like no other ever has.
It's made us stop and think,
About the present and the past.
Though we know we must accept it,
Even though it hurts our hearts.
Only God knows what he puts together,
And what he takes apart

~~ Lupita Almaraz Aguilar

Pain So Deep

Why is the pain so strong?

Why do I feel this way?

Why does it seem so hard?

Why can't I let it fade?

I want to feel good

But I can't or I won't.

I want to smile and laugh

But I don't.

I think if I smile,

I might forget.

Sometimes if I laugh,

I feel guilt and regret.

Why is this pain so deep?

~~Lupita Almaraz Aguilar

Searching

I'm searching for the light
at the end of the tunnel.
But all I can see is a funnel
I think I see it but then it's not there.
I do know why, but I don't want to share.
It is so that they say, you must try.
It is so, but why?

~~ Lupita Almaraz Aguilar

What Was To Come

Nothing could ever prepare us

for all that was to come

The celebration of our love,

When we united us as one.

The most impactful events of our journey

Was the birth of our beautiful girls

The heart-wrenching loss of our daughter,

And when our grandchildren entered our world

It's been a challenge of mega proportions

Much more than we comprehend

We have faltered and failed more times than we know

But we promised to stay till the end

~~ Lupita Almaraz Aguilar

We Love Her So

She said she'd never go

We never thought she would.

We loved her deepest in his hearts,

We loved her all we could.

We love her so

We know the truth.

We love her still.

We thought she knew.

~~ Lupita Almaraz Aguilar

Who Am I?

Who am I —please— may I ask?
I know it's pretty dumb.
But I am lost, and I must say
I don't know where I'm from.
I know but one
And that's myself,
And I need someone
to help.
Whom am I?
I wait to hear.
Can anyone
See me from here?

~~ Lupita Almaraz Aguilar

Chapter 5

There Is Always More

Jinnelle and Tommie are the Author's daughters to whom this chapter is dedicated in representation of the author's vision that "There is Always More."

The author's collection in this chapter is as diverse as it is meaningful.

Though we cannot take it with us when we leave this Earth, we can leave a better version than when she gave us birth.

~~ Lupita Almaraz Aguilar

There Is Always More

I'll be there tomorrow
To search for a better way
To dig a little deeper
Than I did the other day

I'll be there tomorrow
Bringing all my grit
Decipher as I master
More will than there is quit

I'll be there tomorrow
No challenge for persistence
With all the guts and glory
Unchained from all resistance

I'll be there tomorrow
For all who dare to know
To make a bigger impact
Because there is always more.

~~ Lupita Almaraz Aguilar

Miracle

Right in the middle of prayer

The Lord decided to answer our plea

Of course, we know there are miracles

But to witness one is amazing you see.

No real understanding

Of how miracles manifest

But the wonder of it is impacting

And now, we too can attest.

It carries some depth of confusion

But an undeniable truth.

Your thoughts will carry you forward

If you keep your faith resolute.

To Carlos, our wonderful brother – All our Love.

~~Lupita Almaraz Aguilar

A Burden Shared

The future is always unknown
The world is scared and uncertain
Now, more than ever we must be strong
And share this incredible burden

The burden to care for each other
Seems somewhat exhausting at best
But compassion amongst us prevails
And surpasses all the unrest

There shall be reflection to note
A measure of all that we are
As much as we seem disconnected
We now know our world is so small

~~ Lupita Almaraz Aguilar

Maestro's Painting

The woman stood enamored
By the painting on display
Deciphering each stroke
But she seemed somewhat dismayed
She did not want to ask
But gracefully she did,
"Would you be so kind to
elaborate this piece."
The famous artist unamused
Gave a snooty stare
Began to walk away
but then returned with flare.
His tone was calm
As he began to speak
His words as captivating
As was his masterpiece.
Describing every stroke
Of his enormous composition
The creator's explanation
Was a beautiful rendition.
The woman stood in awe
At the maestro's raw emotion
In his elaboration
She witnessed true devotion.

~~Lupita Almaraz Aguilar

Write One For Me?

Don't quite remember

When I started to write

But my thoughts turn to words

As our days turn to night

I go back to the time

When my dad in delight

Would announce what I wrote

And I'd proudly recite

My classmates would ask,

Will you write one for me?

And I'd rush with my pen

To jot what I'd see

I wrote some for them

I wrote some for me

I now write some for you

Take a seat and let's read

~~ Lupita Almaraz Aguilar

The Storm

The storm that appears with a vengeance
Will rattle, destroy, and ravage
The production on such a grand scale
Its delivery more than savage

The loss and the damage so huge
Its wave has a crippling stay
The panic and havoc it causes
Is there for the world on display

But murky waters will clear
Don't underestimate nature
The thunder will roll but then fade
Sun will come sooner or later

~~ Lupita Almaraz Aguilar

Rainmaker

I'm a mover and a shaker
I'm a rainmaker
I'm a moneymaker
I'm not a faker
I'm not a taker

I'm a best friend
I will help you mend
I will defend
Not always with the trend
I don't pretend

I give you my all
carry the ball
I will stand tall
Even when I fall
I will seldom bawl

I've lost big but still strong
Tough times, but keep on
If it goes wrong
Gotta move along
Because I belong.

~~ Lupita Almaraz Aguilar

Conversing With The Moon

Can you illuminate my path
as I walk through this dark night?
Yes, I shall embrace your journey
And share with you my moonlight

I am ever truly grateful
for your kindness Mr. Moon.
Oh, you are quite welcome dear
I do hope to see you soon.

I shall come through in the morning
As I return from my resort.
I travel here each evening
In my quest to find my worth.

Do not cause yourself the anguish,
Mr. Moon will guide your way.
Until you find your courage,
I'll shine this enchanted road each day.

~~ Lupita Almaraz Aguilar

Empowered

Looking back, she smiled.
Empowered and free
No more discussion
No more deceit

Motivated by courage
and self-preservation
She is now a new woman -
A complete transformation

She now sees beyond
A breath of new life
What she did not know
when she was first his bride

Since she found her self-worth
Her future looks bright
All her hard work
She did get it right

~~ Lupita Almaraz Aguilar

God's Words

We loiter, complaining about all we must do
And the burden of work left behind us.
We're constantly asking for help,
But do we ever think of the blind ones?
The Lord once asked if I could move my arms
And with happiness I said, "Yes!"
He then asked if my legs were in motion.
I replied, "It has been for the best."
He thought for a while and then asked me
How much more in life I could do.
I then answered in so much excitement,
And I told him all that I knew.
Thereafter he said,
"Have you thought about others
Who cannot get up from their beds?
Those who lay in depression,
And can't turn their heads?
Have you thought about those
Who can't even learn?
And my dear," he said,
"What more could one want in return?"
I then cried in my thoughts
And replied to his words,
"For the gift of your giving God,
Has been what I've heard."

> *~~Lupita Almaraz Aguilar*

Life

Life is complicated

No way you can explain

For some no tragic will occur

For others there is pain

At times you feel like dying

Sometimes you want to cry

It's not always optimistic

Though you must always try

It may seem at times uncertain

Life can be unkind

Keep a focus on your future

With the positive in mind

~~Lupita Almaraz Aguilar

Holder of Secrets

The holder of a secret

May not hold it long

And if the holder tells it

One might think it's wrong

Now, if the secret must be told

To save someone from harm

Does the holder have a duty

To divulge and ring alarms?

Will you dare to say

What harm deserves disclosure

Then be vulnerable to all

Because you caused the exposure

Regardless of the secret

You may be charged with not to tell

Keeping certain secrets

May not end so well

~~Lupita Almaraz Aguilar

Be A Quilt

Flowers are pretty,

but they will wilt.

Don't be a flower,

if you can be a quilt.

Tall stemmed roses

Are sure to tilt

Don't be a rose

If you can be a quilt

~~Lupita Almaraz Aguilar

Next Chapter

So much work
And not much laughter
All the live-long day
Scoot on over
To the next big chapter
Let nothing in your way

Do it now not later
because later is too late
Move on over
to the next big chapter
Let no one make you wait

~~ Lupita Almaraz Aguilar

Pause

The world demands a little pause
To clear its air of impurity
So, mother nature becomes distraught
Because the masses live with impunity

The backlash of all our actions
Comes charging swift and harsh
The shock is devastating
With an impactful sense of loss

Our inability to care and conserve
Serves up the ultimate consequence
The failure to heed the warnings
Now displaying its evidence

~~ Lupita Almaraz Aguilar

The Night

The night delivers darkness.

You cannot escape its presence.

It too can bring romance.

You cannot ignore its essence.

As its stars can enlighten a moment,

Its darkness can deliver fear.

The night can present such calm,

But can burden a soul with tears.

The night can ravage a moment,

As it can beautifully capture another.

Its moon can shine all its glory,

As its gloom can dreadfully hover.

~~Lupita Almaraz Aguilar

This Chef

This chef throws ingredients together
Knows what to use and what not
He doesn't need to measure
He is the real deal type of big shot

He uses serrano and chili pequin
A dash of black pepper and salt
Crushes comino and garlic
For a heated type of assault

He can whip up a Mexican dish
Better than a Mexican mom
His brisket, fajitas, and ribs
Are all the best barbeque bomb

His steaks are like butter
His cajun cuisine
His pasta and pizza
Like nothing you've seen

Even his baking takes on any baker
Best homemade cookies and cakes
The peach cobbler, pies, and pudding
The best is his Crème Brûlée.

This chef can bring food together
Most food connoisseurs would concede
If you've been so lucky to taste it
Then you most likely agree.

~~Lupita Almaraz Aguilar

The Litigator

He walks into the courtroom

radiating confidence and charm;

Handsome, tall, golden, wavy hair.

He is ready to disarm.

Dark suit, worn cowboy boots,

and an old leather satchel.

More charisma than to which

one should be entitled.

Capturing his audience,

he unwittingly dominates the room.

He makes his mark before he speaks

then, he makes his move.

Judge benched and jury empaneled,

he commands attention.

Unmatched by defense and experts,

He begins his interrogation.

As he cleverly prods,

then shreds, and unravels,

He strikes without warning

and leaves the witnesses baffled.

~~ Lupita Almaraz Aguilar

I'm Going Back Tomorrow

I'm going back tomorrow
To search for a better way
To dig a little deeper
Than I did the other day

Im going back tomorrow
Bringing all my grit
Decipher as I master
More will than there is quit

I'm going back tomorrow
No challenge for persistence
With all the guts and glory
Unchained from all resistance

I'm going back tomorrow
For all who dare to know
To make a bigger impact
Because there is always more.

~~ Lupita Almaraz Aguilar

Acknowledgements

To all who have inspired my writing, I am sincerely grateful.

To my husband, Roy, thank you for thirty-two years of marriage, and for all you have done for me and our family. I am grateful for all the words of encouragement and the praise, and for all the kind critiques. You have always believed in me. All my love.

To my sweet daughter, Jinnelle, thank you for all your love, support, and help with my book. Your input was truly so brilliant!

To my sweet daughter, Tommie, thank you for your love and support. Your kind words on my journey with this book have meant the world to me.

I love my siblings so much. I must say that because of the love and support of my siblings (all eleven of them), and their spouses, I have overcome incredible challenges. Thank you all for everything you have done in supporting me through the celebrations and tribulations, for all the encouragement in my writings, and for giving me more credit than I deserve. A special thanks to my sister, Cecilia Lamar Casas, for all your help with this book. Thank you for listening to me recite a poem every time I needed you.

To my parents, who are both now together with the Lord, thank you for always encouraging me and sharing my poetry with anyone who would listen. I still reminisce about how often my father would proudly ask his brother, my Tio Leonel who lived next door, to listen to me recite one of my poems.

Paulina, you have been with me for so long. When we lost our Nikki, you helped us with Savanna during the most difficult time of our lives. You were probably too young (sixteen) to know how instrumental you were during that period, but you were. My writings in this book reflect this difficult period and I will forever love and cherish you.

Hope, you have been so amazing. As my editor and book publisher, you have made this journey so pleasant. You are inspiring and you are true. The manner in which you deliver critique is that of a true professional. Your candor always on point and refined. Your passion for what you do makes for an unmatched collaboration between us. I am so looking forward to the next one.

~~ Lupita Almaraz Aguilar

I'll Always Remember

I think of you often

Imagine your smile

Your kindness

Your amazing style

The long hours you spent on your hair

Your shyness

Your quirks

How much you cared

Making everyone smile with you

The outbursts of your laughter

The warmth of your hands

The before and after

Mom

~~ Lupita Almaraz Aguilar

Nikki Claudette — Author's daughter
Lost too soon ~~ Forever remembered.

Credits

Photographers:

Photographer: Aria Jace Photography (Author, front and back cover)

Photographer: Gilbert Aguirre, II (Savanna Aguilar, Model)

Photographer: Fernando Aguirre (Mayra Farret, Model)

Photographer: Lupita Almaraz Aguilar (Kayleigh Moses, Model)

Photographer: Jinnelle Veronique Powell (Jinnelle Veronique Powell and Tommie Marie Aguilar, Models)

Photographer: Paulina P. Hernandez (Paulina P. Hernandez, Model)

Models:

Mayra Farrett—Page 11 (TV Personality, Cast Member of Bravo's 'Texicanas' Reality TV Show and Philanthropist. (Photo Title: 'If The Hat Fits' — A classy representation of the Author's writings in Chapter 1)

Kayleigh Moses—Page 53 (Photo Title: 'A Woman Left Alone' — A representation of the Author's writings in Chapter 2)

Paulina P. Hernandez—Page 95 (Photo Title: 'A Lady Laughing' — A representation of the Author's writings in Chapter 3)

Savanna Brhee Aguilar—Page 137 (Photo Title: 'A Daughter Without Her Mother'— The Author's granddaughter, representing the emotion of the Author's writings in Chapter 4)

Jinnelle Veronique Powell and Tommie Marie Aguilar—Page 181 (Photo Title: 'The Future'— The Author's daughters as a representation of the Author's vision that there is always more to say and do as she shares in her writings in Chapter 5)

Hair, Makeup, and Wardrobe:

Patricia Almaraz: Hair Stylist (Author, front and back cover)

Nadia Almaraz: Hair Stylist (Savanna Aguilar, Model Page 137)

Daniella Noehmi Barrera: Makeup (Author, front and back cover; and Savanna Aguilar, Model Page 137)

Cecilia Lamar Casas: Wardrobe Stylist and Collaboration

CPSIA information can be obtained
at www.ICGtesting.com
Printed in the USA
BVHW021251160620
581675BV00007B/24